Lessons on Demand Pre

Teacher Guide and Novel Unit for The Wild Robot

By:

John Pennington

The lessons on demand series is designed to provide ready to use resources for novel study. In this book you will find key vocabulary, student organizer pages, and assessments.

This guide is divided into two sections. Section one is the teacher section which consists of vocabulary and activities. Section two holds all of the student pages, including assessments and graphic organizers.

Now available! Student Workbooks!
Find them on Amazon.com

Section One

Teacher Pages

Vocabulary

Suggested Activities

NAME:

TEACHER:

Date:

Chapters 1-20 Vocabulary

Hurricane

Island

Curiosity

Energy

Wilderness

Artificial

Conserve

Devastation

Instinct

Resin

Camouflage

Observe

Chapters 1-20 Activities

Reading Check Question / Quiz:

Why did Roz end up on the island? A hurricane sent the wreckage to the island

What did Roz find annoying? The pinecones

How did Roz get her energy? From the sun

What did Roz decide to do so that she could survive? Camouflage herself observing the animals behavior.

Blooms Higher Order Question:

Compare how you are like and unlike Roz.

Suggested Activity Sheets (see Section Two):

Character Sketch—Roz

Research Connection—Robot

Research Connection—Ocean

Research Connection—Artificial Intelligence

Draw the Scene

Who, What, When, Where and How

NAME:

TEACHER:

Date:

Chapters 21-39 Vocabulary

Techniques

Agony

Marsupial

Nocturnal

Specialty

Acquaintance

Adopted

Experiment

Ignite

Fertilized

Tranquil

Horizon

Chapters 21-39 Activities

Reading Check Question / Quiz:

What did the animals think of Roz when they first met her? She is a monster

What did Roz do when the geese and their nest was destroyed? She kept the one surviving egg

What name was given to the gooseling? Brightbill

Who helped Roz build a shelter? The beavers

Blooms Higher Order Question:

Create a list of activities the would help you if you became stranded on an island.

Suggested Activity Sheets (see Section Two):

Character Sketch—Loudwing

Character Sketch—Brightbill

Character Sketch—Mr. Beaver

Research Connection—Marsupial

Research Connection—dam

Precognition Sheet

What Would You Do?

NAME:

TEACHER:

Date:

Chapters 40-53 Vocabulary

Survey

Celestial

Atmosphere

Abandon

Adolescent

Predator

Intimidate

Stupor

Parade

Updraft

Hibernation

Migrate

Chapters 40-53 Activities

<u>Reading Check Question / Quiz:</u>

What did Roz and Brightbill see on the ocean when Bightbill learned to fly? A ship

Who did Roz get into a fight with? The young bears

What did Roz need repaired after the fight? Her foot

What did Brightbill need to do now that winter was approaching? Migrate

<u>Blooms Higher Order Question:</u>

Create a list of people and how they help you in your daily life.

<u>Suggested Activity Sheets (see Section Two):</u>

Character Sketch—Shelly

Character Sketch—Nettle and Thorn

Character Sketch—Rockmouth

Character Sketch—Chitchat

Research Connection—Hibernation

Top Ten List—Events

Write a Letter

NAME:

TEACHER:

Date:

Chapter 54-80 Vocabulary

Routine

Respect

Harmonious

Soil

Nourish

Nuisance

Journey

Separation

Celebration

Defective

Resistance

Assault

Chapter 54-80 Activities

Reading Check Question / Quiz:

What woke Roz from her hibernation? The lodge roof fell in letting in sunlight

How did Roz keep the animals alive during the winter? Built more lodges and firepits

What did Roz build to celebrate that a passing ship noticed? A bonfire

Why did Roz need to leave? Because more Reco units would come looking for her

Blooms Higher Order Question:

Develop 10 requirements for being alive.

Suggested Activity Sheets (see Section Two):

Create the Test

Interview

NAME:

TEACHER:

Date:

Chapter Vocabulary

Chapter Activities

Reading Check Question / Quiz:

Blooms Higher Order Question:

Suggested Activity Sheets (see Section Two):

Discussion Questions

Section Two

Student Work Pages

Work Pages

Graphic Organizers

Assessments

Activity Descriptions

Advertisement—Select an item from the text and have the students use text clues to draw an advertisement about that item.

Chapter to Poem—Students select 20 words from the text to write a five line poem with 3 words on each line.

Character Sketch—Students complete the information about a character using text clues.

Comic Strip— Students will create a visual representation of the chapter in a series of drawings.

Compare and Contrast—Select two items to make relationship connections with text support.

Create the Test—have the students use the text to create appropriate test questions.

Draw the Scene—students use text clues to draw a visual representation of the chapter.

Interview— Students design questions you would ask a character in the book and then write that characters response.

Lost Scene—Students use text clues to decide what would happen after a certain place in the story.

Making Connections—students use the text to find two items that are connected and label what kind of relationship connects them.

Precognition Sheet—students envision a character, think about what will happen next, and then determine what the result of that would be.

Activity Descriptions

Pyramid—Students use the text to arrange a series of items in an hierarchy format.

Research Connection—Students use an outside source to learn more about a topic in the text.

Sequencing—students will arrange events in the text in order given a specific context.

Support This! - Students use text to support a specific idea or concept.

Travel Brochure—Students use information in the text to create an informational text about the location

Top Ten List—Students create a list of items ranked from 1 to 10 with a specific theme.

Vocabulary Box—Students explore certain vocabulary words used in the text.

What Would You Do? - Students compare how characters in the text would react and compare that with how they personally would react.

Who, What, When, Where, and How—Students create a series of questions that begin with the following words that are connected to the text.

Write a Letter—Students write a letter to a character in the text.

Activity Descriptions (for scripts and poems)

Add a Character—Students will add a character that does not appear in the scene and create dialog and responses from other characters.

Costume Design—Students will design costumes that are appropriate to the characters in the scene and explain why they chose the design.

Props Needed— Students will make a list of props they believe are needed and justify their choices with text.

Soundtrack! - Students will create a sound track they believe fits the play and justify each song choice.

Stage Directions— Students will decide how the characters should move on, around, or off stage.

Poetry Analysis—Students will determine the plot, theme, setting, subject, tone and important words and phrases.

NAME:

TEACHER:

Date:

Advertisement: Draw an advertisement for the book

NAME:

TEACHER:

Date:

Chapter to Poem

Assignment: Select 20 words found in the chapter to create a poem where each line is 3 words long.

Title:

_____ _____ _____

_____ _____ _____

_____ _____ _____

_____ _____ _____

_____ _____ _____

NAME:

TEACHER:

Date:

Character Sketch

Name

Draw a picture

Personality/ Distinguishing marks

Connections to other characters

Important Actions

NAME:

TEACHER:

Date:

Comic Strip

NAME:

TEACHER:

Date:

Compare and Contrast Venn Diagram

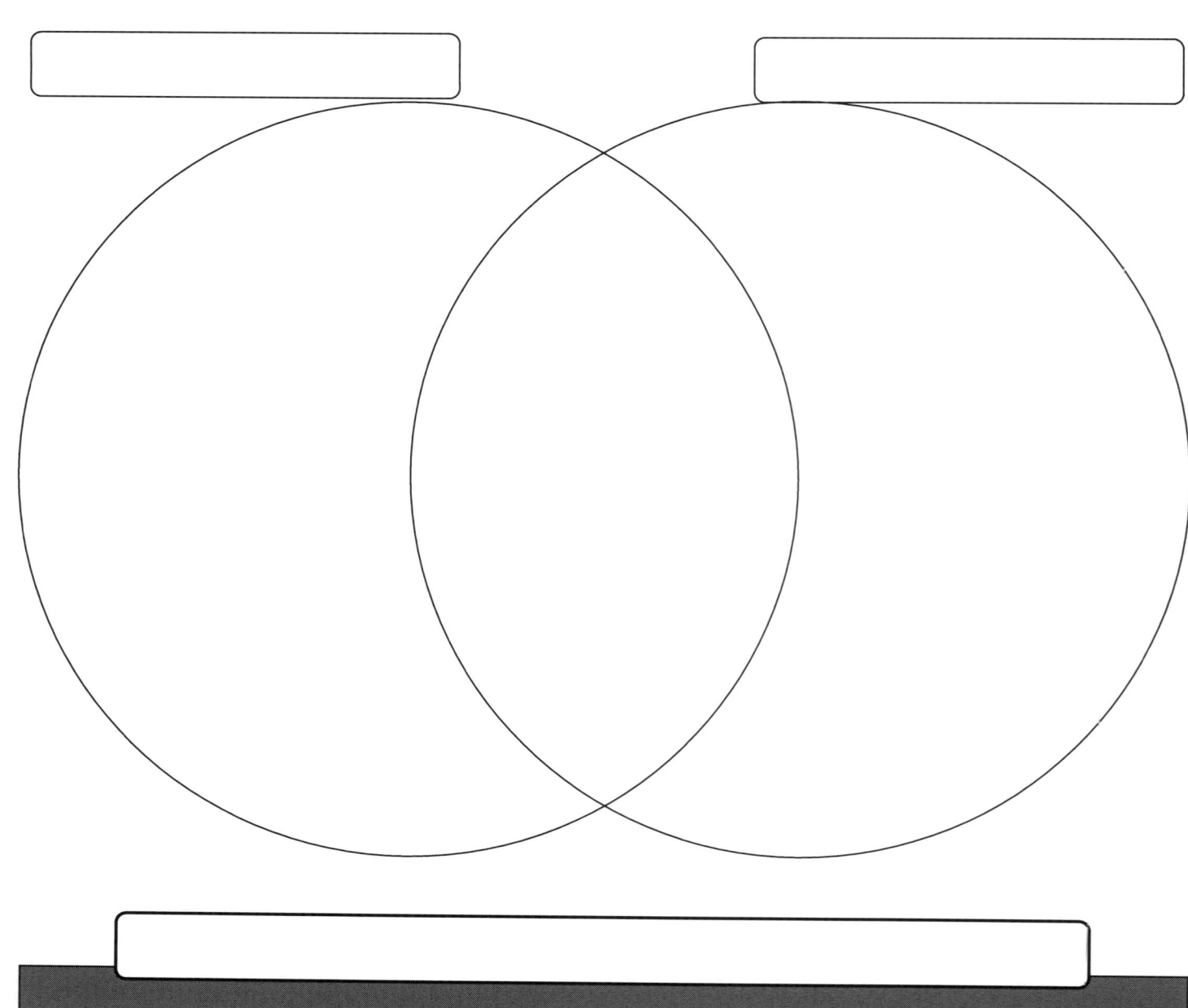

NAME:

TEACHER:

Date:

Create the Test

Question:

Answer:

Question:

Answer:

Question:

Answer:

Question:

Answer:

NAME:

TEACHER:

Date:

Draw the Scene: What five things have you included in the scene?

1 2 3

4 5

NAME:

TEACHER:

Date:

Interview: Who _____

Question:

Answer:

Question:

Answer:

Question:

Answer:

Question:

Answer:

NAME:

TEACHER:

Date:

Lost Scene: Write a scene that takes place between _____ and _____

NAME:

TEACHER:

Date:

Making Connections

What is the connection?

NAME:

TEACHER:

Date:

Precognition Sheet

Who ?

What's going to happen?

What will be the result?

Who ?

What's going to happen?

What will be the result?

Who ?

What's going to happen?

What will be the result?

Who ?

What's going to happen?

What will be the result?

How many did you get correct?

NAME:

TEACHER:

Date:

Assignment: Pyramid

NAME:

TEACHER:

Date:

Research connections

Source (URL, Book, Magazine, Interview)

What am I researching?

Facts I found that could be useful or notes

1.

2.

3.

4.

5.

6.

NAME:

TEACHER:

Date:

Sequencing or timeline

1.

2.

3.

4.

5.

NAME:

TEACHER:

Date:

Support This!

Supporting text

What page?

Supporting text

What page?

Central idea or statement

_____

Supporting text

What page?

Supporting text

What page?

NAME:

TEACHER:

Date:

Travel Brochure

Why should you visit?

What are you going to see?

Map

Special Events

NAME:

TEACHER:

Date:

Top Ten List

1.
2.
3.
4.
5.
6.
7.
8.
9.
10.

NAME:

TEACHER:

Date:

Vocabulary Box

Definition:

Draw:

Word:

Related words:

Use in a sentence:

Definition:

Draw:

Word:

Related words:

Use in a sentence:

NAME:

TEACHER:

Date:

What would you do?

Character: _____

What did they do?

Example from text:

What would you do?

Why would that be better?

Character: _____

What did they do?

Example from text:

What would you do?

Why would that be better?

Character: _____

What did they do?

Example from text:

What would you do?

Why would that be better?

NAME:

TEACHER:

Date:

Who, What, When, Where, and How

Who

What

Where

When

How

NAME:

TEACHER:

Date:

Write a letter

To:

From:

NAME:

TEACHER:

Date:

Assignment:

NAME:

TEACHER:

Date:

Add a Character

Who is the new character?

What reason does the new character have for being there?

Write a dialog between the new character and characters currently in the scene.

You dialog must be 6 lines or more, and can occur in the beginning, middle or end of the scene.

NAME:

TEACHER:

Date:

Costume Design

Draw a costume for one the characters in the scene.

Why do you believe this character should have a costume like this?

NAME:

TEACHER:

Date:

Props Needed

Prop:

What text from the scene supports this?

Prop:

What text from the scene supports this?

Prop:

What text from the scene supports this?

NAME:

TEACHER:

Date:

Soundtrack!

Song:

Why should this song be used?

Song:

Why should this song be used?

Song:

Why should this song be used?

NAME:

TEACHER:

Date:

Stage Directions

List who is moving, how they are moving and use text from the dialog to determine when they move.

Who:

How:

When:

Who:

How:

When:

Who:

How:

When:

NAME:

TEACHER:

Poetry Analysis

Date:

Name of Poem:

Subject:
- Text Support:

Plot:
- Text Support:

Theme:
- Text Support:

Setting:
- Text Support:

Tone:
- Text Support:

Important Words and Phrases:

Why are these words and phrases important:

Made in the USA
Monee, IL
03 February 2021